I0464691

> Occupational Safety and Health Act of 1970
> "To assure safe and healthful working conditions for working men and women; by authorizing enforcement of the standards developed under the Act; by assisting and encouraging the States in their efforts to assure safe and healthful working conditions; by providing for research, information, education, and training in the field of occupational safety and health..."

This publication provides a general overview of worker rights under the *Occupational Safety and Health Act* (OSH Act). This publication does not alter or determine compliance responsibilities which are set forth in OSHA standards and the OSH Act. Moreover, because interpretations and enforcement policy may change over time, for additional guidance on OSHA compliance requirements the reader should consult current administrative interpretations and decisions by the Occupational Safety and Health Review Commission and the courts.

This document, *Workers' Rights*, replaces *Employee Workplace Rights*.

This information will be made available to sensory-impaired individuals upon request. Voice phone: (202) 693-1999; teletypewriter (TTY) number: 1-877-889-5627.

Workers' Rights

U.S. Department of Labor

Occupational Safety and Health Administration

OSHA 3021-09R 2014

U.S. Department of Labor

Contents

Introduction

Worker Protection is the Law of the Land

You have the right to a safe workplace. The *Occupational Safety and Health Act of 1970* (OSH Act) was passed to prevent workers from being killed or otherwise harmed at work. The law requires employers to provide their employees with working conditions that are free of known dangers. The OSH Act created the Occupational Safety and Health Administration (OSHA), which sets and enforces protective workplace safety and health standards. OSHA also provides information, training and assistance to employers and workers.

Contact us if you have questions or want to file a complaint. We will keep your information confidential. **We are here to help you.**

Workers' Rights under the OSH Act

The OSH Act gives workers the right to safe and healthful working conditions. It is the duty of employers to provide workplaces that are free of known dangers that could harm their employees. This law also gives workers important rights to participate in activities to ensure their protection from job hazards. This booklet explains workers' rights to:

- File a confidential complaint with OSHA to have their workplace inspected.
- Receive information and training about hazards, methods to prevent harm, and the OSHA standards that apply to their workplace. The training must be done in a language and vocabulary workers can understand.
- Review records of work-related injuries and illnesses that occur in their workplace.
- Receive copies of the results from tests and monitoring done to find and measure hazards in the workplace.
- Get copies of their workplace medical records.
- Participate in an OSHA inspection and speak in private with the inspector.
- File a complaint with OSHA if they have been retaliated against by their employer as the result of requesting an inspection or using any of their other rights under the OSH Act.

- File a complaint if punished or retaliated against for acting as a "whistleblower" under the additional 21 federal statutes for which OSHA has jurisdiction.

A job must be safe or it cannot be called a good job. OSHA strives to make sure that every worker in the nation goes home unharmed at the end of the workday, the most important right of all.

Employer Responsibilities

Employers have the responsibility to provide a safe workplace. **Employers MUST provide their employees with a workplace that does not have serious hazards and must follow all OSHA safety and health standards.** Employers must find and correct safety and health problems. OSHA further requires that employers must try to eliminate or reduce hazards first by making feasible changes in working conditions – switching to safer chemicals, enclosing processes to trap harmful fumes, or using ventilation systems to clean the air are examples of effective ways to get rid of or minimize risks – rather than just relying on personal protective equipment such as masks, gloves, or earplugs.

Employers **MUST** also:
- Prominently display the official OSHA poster that describes rights and responsibilities under the OSH Act. **This poster is free and can be downloaded from www.osha.gov.**
- Inform workers about hazards through training, labels, alarms, color-coded systems, chemical information sheets and other methods.
- Train workers in a language and vocabulary they can understand.
- Keep accurate records of work-related injuries and illnesses.
- Perform tests in the workplace, such as air sampling, required by some OSHA standards.
- Provide hearing exams or other medical tests required by OSHA standards.
- Post OSHA citations and injury and illness data where workers can see them.
- As of January 1, 2015, notify OSHA within 8 hours of a workplace fatality or within 24 hours of any work-related inpatient hospitalization, amputation or loss of an eye.

- Not retaliate against workers for using their rights under the law, including their right to report a work-related injury or illness.

Who Does OSHA Cover

Private Sector Workers

Most employees in the nation come under OSHA's jurisdiction. OSHA covers most private sector employers and employees in all 50 states, the District of Columbia, and other U.S. jurisdictions either directly through Federal OSHA or through an OSHA-approved state plan. State-run health and safety plans must be at least as effective as the Federal OSHA program. To find the contact information for the OSHA Federal or State Program office nearest you, call 1-800-321-OSHA (6742) or go to www.osha.gov.

State and Local Government Workers

Employees who work for state and local governments are not covered by Federal OSHA, but have OSH Act protections if they work in those states that have an OSHA-approved state plan. The following 22 states or territories have OSHA-approved programs:

Alaska	Arizona	California
Hawaii	Indiana	Iowa
Kentucky	Maryland	Michigan
Minnesota	Nevada	New Mexico
North Carolina	Oregon	South Carolina
Tennessee	Utah	Vermont
Virginia	Washington	Wyoming
Puerto Rico		

Four additional states and one U.S. territory have OSHA-approved plans that cover public sector workers only:

Connecticut	Illinois	New Jersey
New York	Virgin Islands	

Private sector workers in these four states and the Virgin Islands are covered by Federal OSHA.

Federal Government Workers

Federal agencies must have a safety and health program that meets the same standards as private employers. Although OSHA does not fine federal agencies, it does monitor federal agencies and responds to workers' complaints. The United States Postal Service (USPS) is covered by OSHA.

Not Covered under the OSH Act
- Self-employed;
- Immediate family members of farm employers; and
- Workplace hazards regulated by another federal agency (for example, the Mine Safety and Health Administration, the Department of Energy, or Coast Guard).

OSHA-Approved State Plans

☐ OSHA-approved state plans (private sector and public employees)

■ Federal OSHA (private sector and most federal employees)

☐ OSHA-approved state plans (for public employees only; private sector employees are covered by Federal OSHA)

Worker Rights in State-Plan States

States that assume responsibility for their own occupational safety and health programs must have provisions at least as effective as Federal OSHA's, including the protection of worker rights.

Any interested person or group, including employees, with a complaint concerning the operation or administration of a state program may submit a complaint to the appropriate Federal OSHA regional administrator. (See contact list at the end of this booklet). This is called a Complaint About State Program Administration (CASPA). The complaintant's name will be kept confidential. The OSHA regional administrator will investigate all such complaints, and where complaints are found to be valid, require appropriate corrective action on the part of the state.

Right to a Safe and Healthful Workplace

Employers' "General Duty"

Employers have the responsibility to provide a safe and healthful workplace that is free from serious recognized hazards. This is commonly known as the General Duty Clause of the OSH Act.

OSHA Standards: Protection on the Job

OSHA standards are rules that describe the methods that employers must use to protect their employees from hazards. There are four groups of OSHA standards: General Industry, Construction, Maritime, and Agriculture. (General Industry is the set that applies to the largest number of workers and worksites). These standards are designed to protect workers from a wide range of hazards.

These standards also limit the amount of hazardous chemicals, substances, or noise that workers can be exposed to; require the use of certain safe work practices and equipment; and require employers to monitor certain hazards and keep records of workplace injuries and illnesses.

Examples of OSHA standards include requirements to:
- Provide fall protection, such as a safety harness and lifeline;
- Prevent trenching cave-ins;
- Ensure the safety of workers who enter confined spaces such as manholes or grain bins;
- Prevent exposure to high levels of noise that can damage hearing;
- Put guards on machines;
- Prevent exposure to harmful levels of substances like asbestos and lead;
- Provide workers with respirators and other needed safety equipment (in almost all cases, free of charge);

- Provide healthcare workers with needles and sharp instruments that have built-in safety features to prevent skin punctures or cuts that could cause exposure to infectious diseases; and
- Train workers using a language and vocabulary they understand about hazards and how to protect themselves.

Employers must also comply with the General Duty Clause of the OSH Act. This clause requires employers to keep their workplaces free of serious recognized hazards and is generally cited when no specific OSHA standard applies to the hazard.

Right to be Provided Protective Equipment Free of Charge

In some situations it is not possible to completely eliminate a hazard or reduce exposures to a safe level, so respirators, goggles, earplugs, gloves, or other types of personal protective equipment are often used by themselves or in addition to other hazard control measures. Employers must provide most protective equipment free of charge. Employers are responsible for knowing when protective equipment is needed.

Right to Information

OSHA gives workers and their representatives the right to see information that employers collect on hazards in the workplace. Workers have the right to know what hazards are present in the workplace and how to protect themselves. Many OSHA standards require various methods that employers must use to inform their employees, such as warning signs, color-coding, signals, and training. Workers must receive their normal rate of pay to attend training that is required by OSHA standards and rules. The training must be in a language and vocabulary that workers can understand.

Right to Know about Chemical Hazards

The Hazard Communication standard, known as the "right-to-know" standard, requires employers to inform and train workers about hazardous chemicals and substances in the workplace. Employers must:

- Provide workers with effective information and training on hazardous chemicals in their work area.

This training must be in a language and vocabulary that workers can understand;

- Keep a current list of hazardous chemicals that are in the workplace;
- Make sure that hazardous chemical containers are properly labeled with the identity of the hazardous chemical and appropriate hazard warnings; and
- Have and make available to workers and their representatives Safety Data Sheets (SDSs) (formerly known as Material Safety Data Sheets or MSDSs) for each substance that provide detailed information about chemical hazards, their effects, how to prevent exposure, and emergency treatment if an exposure occurs.

Right to Know about Laws and Your Rights

Employers must display the official OSHA Poster, *Job Safety and Health: It's the Law*, in a place where workers will see it. It can be downloaded from the OSHA website, www.osha.gov. Pre-printed copies can also be obtained from OSHA.

Right to Get Copies of Workplace Injury and Illness Records

OSHA's Recordkeeping Rule requires employers in higher-hazard industries with more than ten employees to keep accurate and complete records of work-related injuries and illnesses. (Certain low-hazard workplaces such as offices are not required to keep such records). Employers must record any serious work-related injury or illness on the OSHA Form 300. A serious injury or illness is one that required medical treatment other than first aid, restricted work or days away from work. (Details of each incident are entered on a separate form, the OSHA Form 301). This OSHA Form 300 becomes an ongoing log of all recordable incidents. Each year from February 1 through April 30, employers must post a summary of the injury and illness log from the previous year (OSHA Form 300A) in a place where workers can see it. Workers and their representatives have the right to receive copies of the full OSHA Form 300 log. Following a request, employers must make copies available at the end of the next business day.

These injury and illness logs are important because they provide a comprehensive guide to possible hazards in the workplace that may need correcting. The logs should be used to focus on areas with high injury and illness rates, and to find and fix hazards in order to prevent future occurrences.

Right to Exposure Data

Many OSHA standards require employers to run tests of the workplace environment to find out if their workers are being exposed to harmful levels of hazardous substances such as lead or asbestos, or high levels of noise or radiation. These types of tests are called exposure monitoring. OSHA gives workers the right to get the results of these tests.

Right to Your Medical Records

Some OSHA standards require medical tests to find out if a worker's health has been affected because of exposures at work. For example, employers must test for hearing loss in workers exposed to excessive noise or for decreased lung function in workers exposed to asbestos. Workers have a right to their medical records. Workers' representatives also have a right to review these records but they must first get written permission from the worker to gain access to their medical information.

OSHA Worksite Investigations

OSHA conducts on-site inspections of worksites to enforce the OSHA law that protects workers and their rights. Inspections are initiated without advance notice, conducted using on-site or telephone and facsimile investigations, and performed by highly trained compliance officers. Worksite inspections are conducted based on the following priorities:

- Imminent danger;
- A fatality or hospitalizations;
- Worker complaints and referrals;
- Targeted inspections – particular hazards, high injury rates; and
- Follow-up inspections.

Inspections are conducted without employers knowing when or where they will occur. The employer is not informed in advance that there will be an inspection, regardless of whether it is in response to a complaint or is a programmed inspection.

Right to File a Complaint with OSHA to Request an On-site OSHA Inspection

On-site inspections can be triggered by a worker complaint of a potential workplace hazard or violation. If your workplace has unsafe or unhealthful working conditions, you may want to file a complaint. Often the best and fastest way to get a hazard corrected is to notify your supervisor or employer.

Current workers or their representatives may file a written complaint and ask OSHA to inspect their workplace if they believe there is a serious hazard or that their employer is not following OSHA standards or rules. **Workers and their representatives have the right to ask for an inspection without OSHA telling their employer who filed the complaint.** It is a violation of the OSH Act for an employer to fire, demote, transfer or retaliate in any way against a worker for filing a complaint or using other OSHA rights.

A complaint can be filed in a number of ways:

1. Mail or submit the OSHA Complaint Form – Download the OSHA complaint form from our website (or request a copy from your local OSHA regional or area office), complete it and then fax or mail it back to your nearest OSHA regional or area office. Written complaints that report a serious hazard and are signed by a current worker or representative and submitted to the closest OSHA area office are given priority and are more likely to result in on-site OSHA inspections. A worker or their representative can request (on the form) that OSHA not let their employer know who filed the complaint. Please include your name, address and telephone number so we can contact you to follow up. This information is confidential.

2. Online – Go to the online Complaint Form on the OSHA website, at www.osha.gov/pls/osha7/ eComplaintForm.html. Complaints that are sent in online will most likely be investigated using OSHA's phone/fax system whereby the employer is contacted by phone or fax (not an actual inspection) about the

hazard. **A written complaint that reports a serious hazard and is signed by a current worker(s) or their representative and mailed or otherwise submitted to an OSHA area or regional office is more likely to result in an on-site OSHA inspection.** Complaints received online from workers in OSHA-approved state plan states will be forwarded to the appropriate state plan for response.

3. Telephone – Call your local OSHA regional or area office at 1-800-321-OSHA (6742). OSHA staff can discuss your complaint and respond to any questions you have. **If there is an emergency or the hazard is immediately life-threatening, call your local OSHA regional or area office.**

Who else can file a complaint?

Employee representatives, for the purposes of filing a complaint, are defined as any of the following:

- An authorized representative of the employee bargaining unit, such as a certified or recognized labor organization.
- An attorney acting for an employee.
- Any other person acting in a bona fide representative capacity, including, but not limited to, members of the clergy, social workers, spouses and other family members, health care providers and government officials or nonprofit groups and organizations acting upon specific complaints or injuries from individuals who are employees. In general, the affected employee should have requested, or at least approved, the filing of the complaint on his or her behalf.

In addition, anyone who knows about a workplace safety or health hazard may report unsafe conditions to OSHA, and OSHA will investigate the concerns reported.

Rights of Workers during an Inspection

During an inspection, workers or their representatives have the following rights:

- Have a representative of employees, such as the safety steward of a labor organization, go along on the inspection;
- Talk privately with the inspector; and
- Take part in meetings with the inspector before and after the inspection.

When there is no authorized employee representative, the OSHA inspector must talk confidentially with a reasonable number of workers during the inspection.

Workers are encouraged to:

- Point out hazards;
- Describe injuries or illnesses that resulted from these hazards;
- Discuss past worker complaints about hazards; and
- Inform the inspector of working conditions that are not normal during the inspection.

Following the Inspection

At the end of the inspection, the OSHA inspector will meet with the employer and the employee representatives in a closing conference to discuss any violations found and possible methods by which any hazards found will be abated. If it is not practical to hold a joint conference, the compliance officer will hold separate conferences.

When the OSHA area director determines that there has been a violation of OSHA standards, regulations, or other requirements, the area director issues a citation and notification of proposed penalty to an employer. A citation includes a description of the violation and the date by when the corrective actions must be taken. Depending on the situation, OSHA can classify a violation as serious, willful, or repeat. The employer can also be cited for failing to correct a violation for which it has already been cited. Employers must post a copy of a citation in the workplace where employees will see it.

Workers' Rights following Issuance of Citations

Workers and employers can contest citations once they are issued to the employer. Workers may only contest the amount of time the employer is given to correct the hazard. Workers or their representatives must file a notice of contest with the OSHA area office within 15 days of the issuance of a citation.

Employers have the right to challenge whether there is a violation, how the violation is classified, the amount of any penalty, what the employer must do to correct the violation and how long they have to fix it. Workers or their representatives may participate in this appeals process by electing "party status." This is done by filing a written notice with the Occupational Safety and Health Review Commission (OSHRC).

The OSHRC hears appeals of OSHA citations. They are an independent agency separate from the Department of Labor. For more information, write to:

U.S. Occupational Safety and Health
Review Commission
1120 20th Street NW, 9th Floor
Washington, DC 20036
Phone: 202-606-5400 Fax: 202-606-5050
www.oshrc.gov

Right to Information if No Inspection is Conducted or No Citation Issued

The OSHA area director evaluates complaints from employees or their representatives according to the procedures defined in the OSHA Field Operations Manual. If the area director decides not to inspect the workplace, he or she will send a letter to the complainant explaining the decision and the reasons for it.

OSHA will inform complainants that they have the right to request a review of the decision by the OSHA regional administrator. Similarly, in the event that OSHA decides not to issue a citation after an inspection, employees have a right to further clarification from the area director and an informal review by the regional administrator.

Right to Use Your Rights:
Protection against Retaliation
Whistleblower Protection

The OSH Act prohibits employers from retaliating against their employees for using their rights under the OSH Act. These rights include filing an OSHA complaint, participating in an inspection or talking to the inspector, seeking access to employer exposure and injury records, raising a safety or health issue with the employer, or any other workers' rights described above.

Protection from retaliation means that an employer cannot punish workers by taking "adverse action", such as:

- Firing or laying off;
- Blacklisting;
- Demoting;
- Denying overtime or promotion;
- Disciplining;
- Denying benefits;
- Failing to hire or rehire;
- Intimidation;
- Making threats;
- Reassignment affecting prospects for promotion; or
- Reducing pay or hours.

You can file a complaint alleging retaliation with OSHA if your employer has punished you for using any employee rights established under the OSH Act. **If you have been retaliated against for using your rights, you must file a complaint with OSHA within 30 calendar days from the date the retaliatory decision has been both made and communicated to you (the worker). Contact your local OSHA office by calling, within 30 days of the alleged retaliation, 1-800-321-OSHA (6742), or send a letter to your closest regional or area office. No form is required.** In states with approved state plans, employees may file a complaint with both the State and Federal OSHA.

Following a complaint, OSHA will contact the complainant and conduct an interview to determine whether an investigation is necessary.

If the evidence shows that the employee has been retaliated against for exercising safety and health rights, OSHA will ask the employer to restore that worker's job, earnings, and benefits. If the employer refuses, OSHA may take the employer to court. In such cases, a Department of Labor attorney will represent the employee to obtain this relief.

If There is a Dangerous Situation at Work

If you believe working conditions are unsafe or unhealthful, we recommend that you bring the conditions to your employer's attention, if possible.

You may file a complaint with OSHA concerning a hazardous working condition at any time. However, you should not leave the worksite merely because you have filed a complaint. If the condition clearly presents a risk of death or serious physical harm, there is not sufficient time for OSHA to inspect, and, where possible, you have brought the condition to the attention of your employer, you may have a legal right to refuse to work in a situation in which you would be exposed to the hazard.

If a worker, with no reasonable alternative, refuses in good faith to expose himself or herself to a dangerous condition, he or she would be protected from subsequent retaliation. The condition must be of such a nature that a reasonable person would conclude that there is a real danger of death or serious harm and that there is not enough time to contact OSHA and for OSHA to inspect. Where possible, the employee must have also sought from his employer, and been unable to obtain, a correction of the condition. For more information, go to www.osha.gov/workers.html.

Additional Whistleblower Protections

Since passage of the OSH Act in 1970, Congress has expanded OSHA's whistleblower protection authority to protect workers from retaliation under 22 federal laws. These laws protect employees who report violations of various workplace safety, airline, commercial motor carrier, consumer product, environmental, financial reform, healthcare reform, nuclear, pipeline, public transportation agency, railroad, maritime and securities laws. Complaints must be reported to OSHA within set timeframes following the retaliatory action, as prescribed by each law.

These laws, and the number of days employees have to file a complaint, are:

Worker, Environmental and Nuclear Safety Laws

- *Asbestos Hazard Emergency Response Act (AHERA)* (90 days). Provides retaliation protection for individuals who report violations of environmental laws relating to asbestos in public or private nonprofit elementary and secondary school systems.

- *Clean Air Act (CAA)* (30 days). Provides retaliation protection for employees who, among other things, report violations of this law, which provides for the development and enforcement of standards regarding air quality and air pollution.

- *Comprehensive Environmental Response, Compensation, and Liability Act (CERCLA)* (30 days). Protects employees who report regulatory violations involving accidents, spills, and other emergency releases of pollutants into the environment. The law also protects employees who report violations related to the cleanup of uncontrolled or abandoned hazardous waste sites.

- *Energy Reorganization Act (ERA)* (180 days). Protects certain employees in the nuclear industry who report violations of the Atomic Energy Act (AEA). Protected employees include employees of operators, contractors and subcontractors of nuclear power plants licensed by the Nuclear Regulatory Commission, and employees of contractors working with the Department of Energy under a contract pursuant to the Atomic Energy Act.

- *Federal Water Pollution Control Act (FWPCA) (also known as the Clean Water Act)* (30 days). Provides retaliation protection for employees who, among other things, report violations of the law controlling water pollution.

- *Occupational Safety and Health Act of 1970* (30 days). Provides retaliation protection for employees who exercise a variety of rights guaranteed under this law, such as filing a safety and health complaint with OSHA and participating in an inspection.

- *Safe Drinking Water Act (SDWA)* (30 days).
  Provides retaliation protection for employees
  who, among other things, report violations of this
  law, which requires that all drinking water systems
  assure that their water is potable, as determined
  by the Environmental Protection Agency.

- *Solid Waste Disposal Act (SWDA) (also known
  as the Resource Conservation and Recovery Act)*
  (30 days). Provides retaliation protection for
  employees who, among other things, report
  violations of the law regulating the disposal of
  solid waste.

- *Toxic Substances Control Act (TSCA)* (30 days).
  Provides retaliation protection for employees
  who, among other things, report violations
  of regulations involving the manufacture,
  distribution, and use of certain toxic substances.

Transportation Industry Laws

- *Federal Railroad Safety Act (FRSA)* (180 days).
  Provides protection to employees of railroad
  carriers and contractors and subcontractors of
  those carriers who report an alleged violation
  of any federal law, rule, or regulation relating
  to railroad safety or security, or gross fraud,
  waste, or abuse of federal grants or other public
  funds intended to be used for railroad safety
  or security; report, in good faith, a hazardous
  safety or security condition; refuse to violate
  or assist in the violation of any federal law,
  rule, or regulation relating to railroad safety
  or security; refuse to work when confronted
  by a hazardous safety or security condition
  related to the performance of the employee's
  duties (under imminent danger circumstances);
  request prompt medical or first-aid treatment for
  employment-related injuries; are disciplined for
  requesting medical or first-aid treatment or for
  following an order or treatment plan of a treating
  physician.

- *International Safe Container Act (ISCA)* (60 days).
  Provides retaliation protection for employees
  who report violations of this law, which regulates
  shipping containers.

- *Moving Ahead for Progress in the 21st Century Act (MAP-21)* (180 days). Prohibits retaliation by motor vehicle manufacturers, part suppliers, and dealerships against employees for providing information to the employer or the U.S. Department of Transportation about motor vehicle defects, noncompliance, or violations of the notification or reporting requirements enforced by the National Highway Traffic Safety Administration or for engaging in related protected activities as set forth in the provision.

- *National Transit Systems Security Act (NTSSA)* (180 days). Provides protection to public transit employees who, among other things, report an alleged violation of any federal law, rule, or regulation relating to public transportation agency safety or security, or fraud, waste, or abuse of federal grants or other public funds intended to be used for public transportation safety or security; refuse to violate or assist in the violation of any federal law, rule, or regulation relating to public transportation safety or security; report a hazardous safety or security condition; refuse to work when confronted by a hazardous safety or security condition related to the performance of the employee's duties (under imminent danger circumstances).

- *Pipeline Safety Improvement Act of 2002 (PSIA)* (180 days). Provides retaliation protection for employees who report violations of the federal laws regarding pipeline safety and security or who refuse to violate such provisions.

- *Seaman's Protection Act (SPA)* (180 days). Seamen are protected, among other things, for reporting to the Coast Guard or other federal agency a reasonably believed violation of a maritime safety law or regulation prescribed under that law or regulation. The law also protects work refusals where the employee reasonably believes an assigned task would result in serious injury or impairment of health to the seaman, other seamen, or the public and when the seaman sought, and was unable to obtain correction of the unsafe conditions.

- *Surface Transportation Assistance Act (STAA)* (180 days). Provides retaliation protection for truck drivers and other employees relating to the safety of commercial motor vehicles. Coverage includes all buses for hire and freight trucks with a gross vehicle weight greater than 10,001 pounds.

- *Wendell H. Ford Aviation Investment and Reform Act for the 21st Century (AIR21)* (90 days). Provides retaliation protection for employees of air carriers, contractors, or subcontractors of air carriers who, among other things, raise safety concerns.

Fraud Prevention Laws

- *Affordable Care Act (ACA)* (180 days). Protects employees who report violations of any provision of Title I of the ACA, including but not limited to retaliation based on an individual's receipt of health insurance subsidies, the denial of coverage based on a preexisting condition, or an insurer's failure to rebate a portion of an excess premium.

- *Consumer Financial Protection Act of 2010 (CFPA), Section 1057 of the Dodd-Frank Wall Street Reform and Consumer Protection Act* (180 days). Protects employees who report perceived violations of any provision of the *Dodd-Frank Act*, which encompasses nearly every aspect of the financial services industry. The law also protects employees who report violations of any rule, order, standard or prohibition prescribed by the Bureau of Consumer Financial Protection.

- *Section 806 of the Sarbanes-Oxley Act of 2002 (SOX)* (180 days). Protects employees of certain companies who report alleged mail, wire, bank or securities fraud; violations of the Securities and Exchange Commission (SEC) rules and regulations; or violations of Federal laws related to fraud against shareholders. The law covers employees of publicly traded companies and companies required to file certain reports with the SEC.

Consumer Safety Laws

- *Consumer Product Safety Improvement Act (CPSIA)* (180 days). Protects employees who report to their employer, the federal government, or a state attorney general reasonably perceived violations of any statute or regulation within the jurisdiction of the Consumer Product Safety Commission (CPSC). CPSIA covers employees of consumer product manufacturers, importers, distributors, retailers, and private labelers.

- *FDA Food Safety Modernization Act (FSMA)* (180 days). Protects employees of food manufacturers, distributors, packers, and transporters for reporting a violation of the Food, Drug, and Cosmetic Act, or a regulation promulgated under this law. Employees are also protected from retaliation for refusing to participate in a practice that violates this law.

If you believe that you have been retaliated against, call 1-800-321-OSHA (6742) to be connected to the nearest OSHA office to report your complaint. For more information, visit OSHA's Whistleblower page at www.whistleblowers.gov.

OSHA Assistance, Services and Programs

OSHA has a great deal of information to assist employers in complying with their responsibilities under OSHA law. Several OSHA programs and services can help employers identify and correct job hazards, as well as improve their injury and illness prevention program.

Establishing an Injury and Illness Prevention Program

The key to a safe and healthful work environment is a comprehensive injury and illness prevention program.

Injury and illness prevention programs are systems that can substantially reduce the number and severity of workplace injuries and illnesses, while reducing costs to employers. Thousands of employers across the United States already manage safety using injury and illness prevention programs, and OSHA believes that all employers can and should do the same. Thirty-four states have requirements or voluntary guidelines for workplace injury and illness prevention programs. Most successful injury and illness prevention programs are based on a common set of key elements. These include management leadership, worker participation, hazard identification, hazard prevention and control, education and training, and program evaluation and improvement. Visit OSHA's Injury and Illness Prevention Programs web page at www.osha.gov/dsg/topics/safetyhealth for more information.

Compliance Assistance Specialists

OSHA has compliance assistance specialists throughout the nation located in most OSHA offices. Compliance assistance specialists can provide information to employers and workers about OSHA standards, short educational programs on specific hazards or OSHA rights and responsibilities, and information on additional compliance assistance resources. For more details, visit www.osha.gov/dcsp/compliance_assistance/cas.html or call 1-800-321-OSHA (6742) to contact your local OSHA office.

Free On-site Safety and Health Consultation Services for Small Business

OSHA's On-site Consultation Program offers free and confidential advice to small and medium-sized businesses in all states across the country, with priority given to high-hazard worksites. Each year, responding to requests from small employers looking to create or improve their safety and health management programs, OSHA's On-site Consultation Program conducts over 29,000 visits to small business worksites covering over 1.5 million workers across the nation.

On-site consultation services are separate from enforcement and do not result in penalties or citations. Consultants from state agencies or universities work with employers to identify workplace hazards, provide advice on compliance with OSHA standards, and assist in establishing safety and health management programs.

For more information, to find the local On-site Consultation office in your state, or to request a brochure on consultation services, visit www.osha.gov/consultation, or call 1-800-321-OSHA (6742).

Under the consultation program, certain exemplary employers may request participation in OSHA's **Safety and Health Achievement Recognition Program (SHARP)**. Eligibility for participation includes, but is not limited to, receiving a full-service, comprehensive consultation visit, correcting all identified hazards and developing an effective safety and health management program. Worksites that receive SHARP recognition are exempt from programmed inspections during the period that the SHARP certification is valid.

Cooperative Programs

OSHA offers cooperative programs under which businesses, labor groups and other organizations can work cooperatively with OSHA. To find out more about any of the following programs, visit www.osha.gov/dcsp/compliance_assistance/index_programs.html.

Strategic Partnerships and Alliances
The OSHA Strategic Partnerships (OSP) provide the opportunity for OSHA to partner with employers, workers, professional or trade associations, labor organizations, and/or other interested stakeholders. OSHA Partnerships are formalized through unique agreements designed to encourage, assist, and recognize partner efforts to eliminate serious hazards and achieve model workplace safety and health practices. Through the Alliance Program, OSHA works with groups committed to worker safety and health to prevent workplace fatalities, injuries and illnesses by developing compliance assistance tools and resources to share with workers and employers, and educate workers and employers about their rights and responsibilities.

Voluntary Protection Programs (VPP)
The VPP recognize employers and workers in private industry and federal agencies who have implemented effective safety and health management programs and maintain injury and illness rates below the national average for their respective industries. In VPP, management, labor, and OSHA work cooperatively

and proactively to prevent fatalities, injuries, and illnesses through a system focused on: hazard prevention and control, worksite analysis, training, and management commitment and worker involvement.

Occupational Safety and Health Training

The OSHA Training Institute in Arlington Heights, Illinois, provides basic and advanced training and education in safety and health for federal and state compliance officers, state consultants, other federal agency personnel and private sector employers, workers, and their representatives. In addition, 27 OSHA Training Institute Education Centers at 42 locations throughout the United States deliver courses on OSHA standards and occupational safety and health issues to thousands of students a year.

For more information on training, contact the OSHA Directorate of Training and Education, 2020 Arlington Heights Road, Arlington Heights, IL 60005; call 1-847-297-4810; or visit www.osha.gov/otiec.

OSHA Educational Materials

OSHA has many types of educational materials in English, Spanish, Vietnamese and other languages available in print or online. These include:

- Brochures/booklets that cover a wide variety of job hazards and other topics;
- Fact Sheets, which contain basic background information on safety and health hazards;
- Guidance documents that provide detailed examinations of specific safety and health issues;
- Online Safety and Health Topics pages;
- Posters;
- Small, laminated QuickCards™ that provide brief safety and health information; and
- *QuickTakes*, OSHA's free, twice-monthly online newsletter with the latest news about OSHA initiatives and products to assist employers and workers in finding and preventing workplace hazards. To sign up for *QuickTakes* visit www.osha.gov/quicktakes.

To view materials available online or for a listing of free publications, visit www.osha.gov/publications. You can also call 1-800-321-OSHA (6742) to order publications.

OSHA's website also has a variety of eTools. These include utilities such as expert advisors, electronic compliance assistance, videos and other information for employers and workers. To learn more about OSHA's safety and health tools online, visit www.osha.gov.

NIOSH Health Hazard Evaluation Program
Getting Help with Health Hazards
The National Institute for Occupational Safety and Health (NIOSH) is a federal agency that conducts scientific and medical research on workers' safety and health. At no cost to employers or workers, NIOSH can help identify health hazards and recommend ways to reduce or eliminate those hazards in the workplace through its Health Hazard Evaluation (HHE) Program.

Workers, union representatives and employers can request a NIOSH HHE. An HHE is often requested when there is a higher than expected rate of a disease or injury in a group of workers. These situations may be the result of an unknown cause, a new hazard, or a mixture of sources. To request a NIOSH Health Hazard Evaluation go to www.cdc.gov/niosh/hhe/request.html. To find out more about the Health Hazard Evaluation Program:

- Call (513) 841-4382, or to talk to a staff member in Spanish, call (513) 841-4439; or

- Send an email to HHERequestHelp@cdc.gov.

How to Contact OSHA

For questions or to get information or advice, to report an emergency, report a fatality or catastrophe, order publications, sign up for OSHA's e-newsletter *QuickTakes*, or to file a confidential complaint, contact your nearest OSHA office, visit www.osha.gov or call OSHA at 1-800-321-OSHA (6742), TTY 1-877-889-5627.

For assistance, contact us.

We are OSHA. We can help.

It's confidential.

OSHA Regional Offices

Region I
Boston Regional Office
(CT*, ME, MA, NH, RI, VT*)
JFK Federal Building, Room E340
Boston, MA 02203
(617) 565-9860 (617) 565-9827 Fax

Region II
New York Regional Office
(NJ*, NY*, PR*, VI*)
201 Varick Street, Room 670
New York, NY 10014
(212) 337-2378 (212) 337-2371 Fax

Region III
Philadelphia Regional Office
(DE, DC, MD*, PA, VA*, WV)
The Curtis Center
170 S. Independence Mall West
Suite 740 West
Philadelphia, PA 19106-3309
(215) 861-4900 (215) 861-4904 Fax

Region IV
Atlanta Regional Office
(AL, FL, GA, KY*, MS, NC*, SC*, TN*)
61 Forsyth Street, SW, Room 6T50
Atlanta, GA 30303
(678) 237-0400 (678) 237-0447 Fax

Region V
Chicago Regional Office
(IL*, IN*, MI*, MN*, OH, WI)
230 South Dearborn Street
Room 3244
Chicago, IL 60604
(312) 353-2220 (312) 353-7774 Fax

Region VI
Dallas Regional Office
(AR, LA, NM*, OK, TX)
525 Griffin Street, Room 602
Dallas, TX 75202
(972) 850-4145 (972) 850-4149 Fax
(972) 850-4150 FSO Fax

Region VII
Kansas City Regional Office
(IA*, KS, MO, NE)
Two Pershing Square Building
2300 Main Street, Suite 1010
Kansas City, MO 64108-2416
(816) 283-8745 (816) 283-0547 Fax

Region VIII
Denver Regional Office
(CO, MT, ND, SD, UT*, WY*)
Cesar Chavez Memorial Building
1244 Speer Boulevard, Suite 551
Denver, CO 80204
(720) 264-6550 (720) 264-6585 Fax

Region IX
San Francisco Regional Office
(AZ*, CA*, HI*, NV*, and American Samoa,
Guam and the Northern Mariana Islands)
90 7th Street, Suite 18100
San Francisco, CA 94103
(415) 625-2547 (415) 625-2534 Fax

Region X
Seattle Regional Office
(AK*, ID, OR*, WA*)
300 Fifth Avenue, Suite 1280
Seattle, WA 98104
(206) 757-6700 (206) 757-6705 Fax

* These states and territories operate their own
OSHA-approved job safety and health plans and
cover state and local government employees as well
as private sector employees. The Connecticut, Illinois,
New Jersey, New York and Virgin Islands programs
cover public employees only. (Private sector workers
in these states are covered by Federal OSHA). States
with approved programs must have standards that
are identical to, or at least as effective as, the Federal
OSHA standards.

Note: To get contact information for OSHA area
offices, OSHA-approved state plans and OSHA
consultation projects, please visit us online at
www.osha.gov or call us at 1-800-321-OSHA (6742).